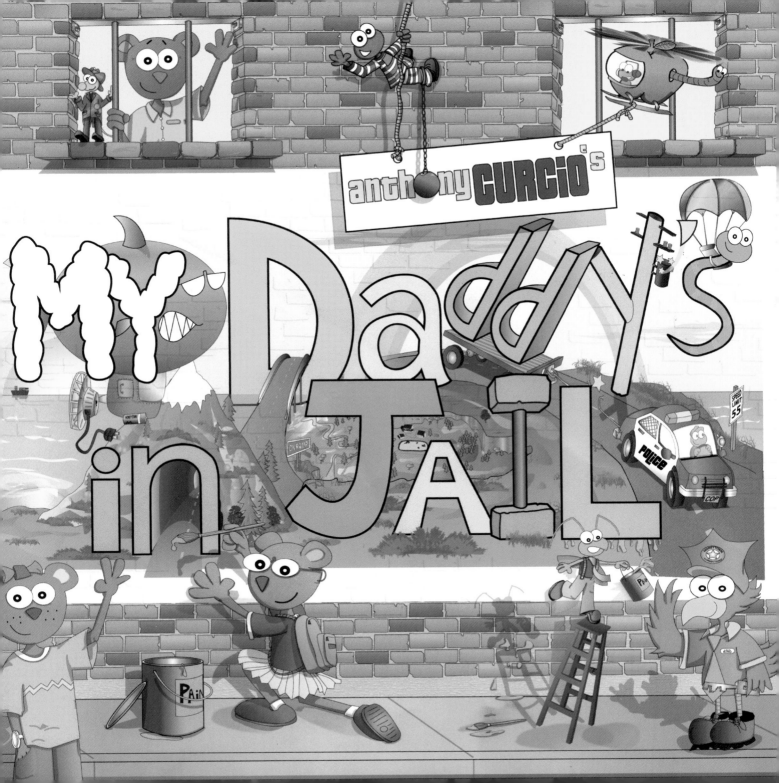

ISBN 978-0-692-47043-5

Have you seen this ant?
He is hiding on every page.

Can you help us find him?

Emergency! Emergency! Everywhere a frown.
Don't they know to smile? This is Honeytown!

I'm Rhymer Roach. I was called to this scene,
To find out why everyone's being so mean!

Just look at these kids at
The Honeytown School!

How many can you find that
are breaking a rule?

Grown-ups have rules too,
Only their's are called laws.

And adults break rules also
(even they have their flaws).

I found 15.

Hey! There he is!

Kids that break the rules are sent to this wall where they pout.
Adults that break laws go to jail, like a grown-up timeout.

What do they eat, where do they sleep at this jail place they go?

My bear friends have a dad there,
So these answers they should know.

Rhymer's blowing up his shark blimp so he can be on his way,
To meet the Bears at Honeytown Jail and see what they have to say.

I fly my blimp high, far from cats and their sharp claws!

Although flying blimps in the city is against one of Honeytown's laws.

As Rhymer waits for his blimp to inflate, he watches some TV.

No sharing, no caring, is all that I see.

Who acts like this, who even would?

They're not treating others the way that they should.

If they break a big law or commit a bad crime,

They'll get hauled off to jail where they'll do some hard time.

And I'd have to conclude, from the looks on these faces,
That jail surely isn't the nicest of places.

They call *this* the big house?

Greenie the Ant

Rhymer's friends Bella and Lyla are already there.
See their Daddy waving? He's the brown bear!

Now I'm a good roach. Me in jail? No way!
These are bad animals. That's what I always say.

The Bears write letters,
They talk on the phone,

But sometimes they get sad
and feel all alone.

If you feel sad there's only one thing to do:
Remember this carefully, your Daddy loves you!

While flying there, Rhymer ignored this sign.

Crashed his shark blimp, then said he was fine.

Too bad
his blimp
hit Greenie
the Ant on
his head.

Greenie would not have been hurt if I had just stopped and read!

You are unique. No one else has a fingerprint like you!

The food isn't good and it's served by a guard.
The beds aren't soft, they are very, very hard.

This is nothing at all like your comfortable house.
Just ask that snoring little mouse!

Inside this place sure isn't any fun!
Who'd want to be somewhere there isn't any sun?

I cried, I kicked, but now I'm in here too!
I guess I'm just like these bad animals in this jail of a zoo.

It's like a grown-up timeout, but a little more sad.
You ask someone in jail, they'd wish they hadn't done something bad!

All this fun stuff that animals in jail can't do,

But the worst part for them is they aren't free like you.

Bella and Lyla Bear's Daddy only thinks about one thing.

Going home to his special girls - just the thought makes him sing!

This is torture! Make him stop!

Most animals spend time dreaming of the day,

When they can be with their families again, have fun and play.

Oh no! Help!

Rhymer's behind that big thinking bubble.

That cat looks hungry!

Rhymer's in some really **BIG** trouble!

"HELP! HELP!" is what Rhymer yelped.

To correct what he just heard,
Up jumped the Jail-Bird.

These animals are good for goodness sakes!
Sometimes good animals just make bad mistakes!

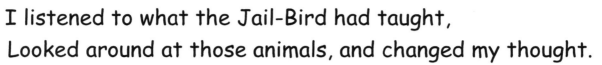

I listened to what the Jail-Bird had taught,
Looked around at those animals, and changed my thought.

After that, me and kitty made peace.

Then I heard it was time for my release.

My best shirt, my best pants -
Do you like the brown?

Today is a big day! I'm all smiles
and no frown!

I'm so happy! I'm so excited!
I flipped upside down!

No more jails, no more visiting rooms, or feeling all alone.
It was sad and it was hard but now our Daddy is home.

Remember you are loved - yes I mean YOU!
Things aren't always easy but you will get through.

As for me?

I'm a cockroach and don't always act nice.

But after going to jail...
Now I think twice!

This book is dedicated to:

ISABELLA
and
LYLA

The two beary best girls a daddy could ever have.

CPSIA information can be obtained at www.ICGtesting.com
Printed in the USA
LVIW01n0900160917
548564LV00001B/5